YOUR KNOWLEDGE HAS VALUE

- We will publish your bachelor's and
  master's thesis, essays and papers

- Your own eBook and book -
  sold worldwide in all relevant shops

- Earn money with each sale

Upload your text at www.GRIN.com
and publish for free

Tom McKaskill

Make Millions From Your Business

101 tips for success

GRIN Verlag

Bibliografische Information der Deutschen Nationalbibliothek:

Die Deutsche Bibliothek verzeichnet diese Publikation in der Deutschen National-
bibliografie; detaillierte bibliografische Daten sind im Internet über http://dnb.d-
nb.de/ abrufbar.

Imprint:

Copyright © 2011 GRIN Verlag GmbH
Druck und Bindung: Books on Demand GmbH, Norderstedt Germany
ISBN: 978-3-640-91675-7

This book at GRIN:

http://www.grin.com/en/e-book/171994/make-millions-from-your-business

GRIN - Your knowledge has value

Der GRIN Verlag publiziert seit 1998 wissenschaftliche Arbeiten von Studenten, Hochschullehrern und anderen Akademikern als eBook und gedrucktes Buch. Die Verlagswebsite www.grin.com ist die ideale Plattform zur Veröffentlichung von Hausarbeiten, Abschlussarbeiten, wissenschaftlichen Aufsätzen, Dissertationen und Fachbüchern.

Visit us on the internet:

http://www.grin.com/

http://www.facebook.com/grincom

http://www.twitter.com/grin_com

Dr. Tom McKaskill

MAKE MILLIONS FROM YOUR BUSINESS

101 Tips For Success

BREAKTHROUGH PUBLICATIONS

Contents

KINDLE BOOKS BY DR. TOM MCKASKILL

Insights

The majority of muti-millionaires have participated in the sale or listing of an entrepreneurial business.

Whether you are an entrepreneur or simply a key employee, you have a greater chance of accumulating wealth through a startup than via a salary.

Most early stage firms fail from a lack of basic business acumen. Easily fixed if you are prepared to spend the time undertaking some business education.

Success in business is mostly common sense. Combine that with some experience and wisdom and you have a good chance of success.

While luck always plays a part in any success story, attention to detail and a deliberate strategy will greatly improve the probability of success.

DR. TOM MCKASKILL

Global serial entrepreneur, consultant, educator and author, Dr. McKaskill has established a reputation for providing insights into how entrepreneurs start, develop and harvest their ventures. Acknowledged as the world's leading authority on exit strategies for high growth enterprises, Dr. McKaskill provides both real world experience with a professional educator's talent for explaining complex management problems that confront entrepreneurs. His talent for teaching executives and his pragmatic approach to management education has gained him a reputation as a popular speaker at conferences, workshops and seminars. His approaches to building sustainable, profitable ventures and to selling businesses at a significant premium, has gained him considerable respect within the entrepreneurial community.

Upon completing his doctorate at London Business School, Dr. McKaskill worked as a management consultant, later co-founding Pioneer Computer Systems in Northampton, UK. After being its President for 13 years, it was sold to Ross Systems Inc. During his tenure at Pioneer, the company grew from 3 to 160 people with offices in England, New Zealand and USA, raised venture capital, undertook two acquisitions and acquired over 2,000 customers. Following the sale of Pioneer to Ross Systems, Dr. McKaskill stayed with Ross for three years and then left to form another company, Distinction Software Inc. In 1997 Atlanta based Distinction raised $US 2 million in venture capital and after five years, with a staff of 30, a subsidiary in New Zealand and distributors in five countries, was sold to Peoplesoft Inc. In 1994 Dr. McKaskill started a consulting business in Kansas which was successfully sold in the following year.

After a year as visiting Professor of International Business at Georgia State University, Dr. McKaskill was appointed Professor of Entrepreneurship at the Australian Graduate School of Entrepreneurship (AGSE) in June 2001. Professor McKaskill was the Academic Director of the Master of Entrepreneurship and Innovation program at AGSE for the following 5 years. In 2006 Dr. McKaskill was appointed the Richard Pratt Chair in Entrepreneurship at AGSE. Dr. McKaskill retired from Swinburne University in February 2008.

Dr. McKaskill is the author of eight published paperback books for entrepreneurs covering such topics as new venture growth, raising venture capital, selling a business, acquisitions strategy and angel investing. He conducts workshops and seminars on these topics for entrepreneurs around the world. He has conducted workshops and seminars for educational institutions, associations, private firms and public corporations, including KPMG, St George Bank, AMP, AICD and PWC. Dr. McKaskill is a successful columnist and writer for popular business magazines and entrepreneur portals.

To assist Angel and Venture Capital investors create strategic exits for their investee firms, Dr. McKaskill conducts seminars, workshops and individual strategy sessions for the investor and their investee management teams.

Dr. McKaskill completed 18 e-books for worldwide distribution. He has also produced over 150 YouTube videos to assist entrepreneurs develop and exit their ventures.

Tom McKaskill is a member of the Brisbane and Melbourne Angel Groups and of the Australian Association of Angel Investors.

Dr. Tom McKaskill
Australia
May 2011

info@tommckaskill.com
www.tommckaskill.com

Published by:
Breakthrough Publications
RBN: B2173298N
Level 1, 75A Chapel St.,
Windsor, Melbourne, VIC 3181

www.tommckaskill.com
Copyright © 2011 Tom McKaskill

McKaskill, Tom
Make Millions From Your Business - 101 tips for success

ISBN: 978-0-9870872-7-0 (116 pages) 245H x 175W
1. Business enterprises. 2. Success in business. 3. Entrepreneurship.

Cover design: T. McKaskill
Page design and production: T. McKaskill

INTRODUCTION

What does it take to become a multi-millionaire?

Most people would say 'Win a lottery?' But how many people do that – very few. Maybe the chances are 1 in several million. Then you could always try the 'get rich quick schemes' where the only people who make the money seem to be the promoters. Of course, you could always do day trading on the stock exchange where it seems 99% of the traders lose their money and only a very small number manage to make an average salary.

You could always do some property speculation but few people would take that on after the horrendous losses over the GFC. Some do take a lifetime to build a rental portfolio and that does show that a long and consistent pattern of investment can make a difference but few have the discipline to see it through.

What is interesting is to look at the data. Who are the multi-millionaires (if we exclude the insignificant numbers of lottery winners, gamblers and speculators)?

The data is revealing. Only about 0.7% of the populations of the USA, UK and Australia have net worth of US$1 million dollars or more. However, these days $1 million doesn't achieve much. Where you need to be is in the multi-millionaire group. Clearly that percentage is going to be much lower. (Source: World Wealth Report 2010, Capgemini)

Those who inherent wealth only make up about 5% of the wealthy. The next largest group are those who have accumulated wealth through high salaries. They make up 15% of the wealthy. But, by far, the largest group are those who have made their wealth by building a business or in participating in the exit of a business – a trade sale or an initial public offering. This group make up 80% of the multi-millionaire class.

According to Fabio Marciano in his paper 'The 21 Habits of Multi-Millionaires' :

"While 20% of the wealthy are retirees, more than 2/3rds of the rest own their own businesses. The self-employed are four times more likely to be millionaires than those who work for others." He also states "Usually the wealthy individual is a businessman who has lived in the same town for all of his adult life. This person owns a small factory, a chain of stores, or a service company."

(source: www.fabmansecrets.com)

Who are these people?

Generally the people who make money from the sale or listing of a business represent several groups of people.

- *Founders* – those who start new ventures. These are the entrepreneurs.
- *Senior Executives* – these are the individuals who have equity or share options.
- *Key Employees* – a few critical employees will have shares or options.
- *Investors* – these are founding investors, angel investors or venture capital fund managers and investors.

So it is not just the entrepreneurs who cash up, it is also often those who are in the management team and their investors. Even a small firm of 30 staff might have 3 – 5 individuals who cash out at multi-million dollar values. The others might also have shares or options which provide them with payouts in the tens if not hundreds of thousands of dollars.

What is the probability?

Actually the chances of being part of a private business which has a value in excess of a few million dollars is reasonably good compared to the chances of winning the lottery.

If we assume that any business which employs more than 20 people has a value in excess of $2 million, the probability of at least one individual receiving $2 million or more is good. Data from both the USA and Australia show that the number of firms exceeding this threshold is about 10%.

The US Census Bureau data for 2008 estimates there are a total number of firms of 5,930,132, of which approximately 524,000 firms have between 20 and 99 employees (8.8%) and a further 89,000 have 100 – 499 employees (1.5%).

(Source: http://www.sba.gov/advocacy/849/12162)

In the ABS report for 1997 there were 78,304 (9%) businesses with 20-199 employees and 5,876 (<1%) businesses with 200 or more employees.

Only 121,557 (6%) businesses had turnover above $2m per annum.

(Source: Australian Bureau of Statistics 8165.0 - Counts of Australian Businesses, including Entries and Exits, Jun 2003 to Jun 2007)

Working out how many millionaires this sector of society could generate is somewhat speculative but worth a guess. There are about 7.8 million households in Australia for a population of about 22.5 million people. Let us assume that 15% of these households are retired folks. That leaves us with about 6.6 million households with employed adults. If each of our businesses with more than 20 employees contributed 3 millionaires, this would give us about 252,000 millionaires for our 6.6 million households or a probability of 3.8%. So you have a 1 in 26 chance of becoming a millionaire. Compared to the general population, this gives you a 4 times better chance of making it into the Millionaires Club. That certainly beats the lottery, gambling or day trading.

What do you need to do?

- Start a business
- Join a business as a senior executive.
- Become a key employee.
- Invest in a startup business.
- Become an angel investor.

However, being in business is not without its risk which is why few attain the size needed to provide their stakeholders with significant wealth on exit.

The ABS data provide the following rate of exits of new ventures; 18% exit after 2 years, 24% after 3 years, 35% after 5 years, 55% after 10 years and 65% after 15 years.

(Source: 1997 ABS report of business exits in Australia)

However, while this data generally refers to failures or business closure, an exit could include the sale of the business, so these probabilities somewhat overstate failure rates.

What is clearly obvious is that people who get involved in early stage firms have a much higher chance of gaining significant wealth. This does not only apply to the founding entrepreneur but to those who actively support him/her during the early phase of the venture. There are many examples of successful entrepreneurial ventures where tens and hundreds of employees and investors secured signifiant wealth. Even in smaller enterprises, several individuals can walk away with multi millions. The decision is yours - but don't hestitate. This is a great opportunity to change your life forever.

THE 101 TIPS FOR SUCCESS

While failure rates for early stage ventures are reasonably high, most fail because they lack the fundamentals of a good business. Most businesses fail because the business idea was never properly researched, the founder lacked any business training or they had inadequate funding to see their business through the early development stage.

Avoiding the basic mistakes, ensuring you have some business education and learning from the mistakes of others, substantially increases the likelihood of success.

In this book I have set out what I consider to be the 101 rules for survival, growth and profitability of a business. It comes from twenty years of practical experience in a series of early stage ventures, a deep understanding of entrepreneurship from seven years as a Professor of Entrepreneurship and many years as a mentor and coach to a wide range of entrepreneurial ventures.

Your best chance of joining the Millionaires Club is to be part of an entrepreneurial venture and follow my 101 tips for success.

1. Begin With The End In Mind

There are many things we do in business which take years to come to fruition. Without a plan to make it happen it is highly unlikely we will achieve our personal and business objectives. Start with what you want from the business – security, status, wealth, interesting and challenging activities and so on. With the end in mind, you have a way of judging every decision you make. Does it advance you towards your goal or is a distraction?

You need to set out what you want the business to look like in 1, 3 and 5 years time and then build a plan to get you there. Even if it is your intention to sell the business, work out who the best buyers are and what you need to do to make it a great deal for them. Make your goal realistic but challenging. Set out the intermediate steps you need to achieve and use these to measure progress. But don't be a slave to the plan. If a better opportunity comes along, be open to evaluating it against your prior goal.

2. Hire The Best

Good people are hard to find and often difficult to hold onto. But good people are effective. They get the job done, often in half the time. They need less supervision and often take initiative. They don't leave a mess behind them which wastes your own time fixing. They are good to work with as they get on with the job. They lift the productivity of those around them and make being in business worthwhile.

On the other hand, there are people who you put up with. They scrape through, never doing the job really the way you would like, requiring a lot of hand holding and leaving a few problems in their wake. You often wonder why you put up with them but you accept that they are better than no one. In the end, you compromise your business because you end up with accepting mediocrity. In hindsight, the best people are worth having even if they only stay for a short period.

3. Share The Wealth

Entrepreneurs create organizations which, if they are successful, are only so because of the combined efforts of all the employees. Rewarding those who contributed is a great way to say thanks. It also is a motivating force for all those who turn up every day to make it happen.

The values which underpin an organization says a lot about the founders and much about the way in which the organization works. There is a big difference between working for 'you' and working for 'us. You need to ask yourself what you would like to happen if times were tough - will everyone pull together or will people desert for the security of a larger company?

What reputation do you want as an entrepreneur? Remember that the successful ones will often have more than one venture. Imagine how much easier it will be to recruit the right people when you have a reputation for sharing the wealth.

4. Have A Consistent Message

Have you ever taken a good hard look at your marketing and sales literature and asked the questions 'Who are we?' What do we do? and 'Who are our customers?'. You will be surprised how confusing the messages are. Different people over time make up their own version of the corporate message creating a very confusing picture.

If your own people can't get the message right, imagine how difficult it is for your customers, suppliers, service providers and recruiters. Consider the potential customers - what do they see as they review your marketing material?

You need to move to a state where the messages are consistent in all your published material but also your stakeholders all have the same view of what you do.

5. Keep Fit and Healthy

Creating a successful business is a marathon not a stroll in the park. Not only do you have to survive the experience to collect the rewards and enjoy them but you carry the responsibility of everyone who works for you every day. You owe it to your family, employees, customers and shareholders to be available to do your job, You also need to be alert and have the energy to cope with the stresses which come with the job.

The journey of the entrepreneur is a roller coaster and it will have more than its fair share of challenges. There will be long days and nights, times of stress and despair but interspersed with moments of sheer joy when things go right. While you don't need to be a gym junkie or a health nut, you do need to acknowledge that a lot of people depend on you for leadership, vision and support through the good times and the bad times.

6. Hire Slow – Fire Fast

The hardest lesson to learn in business is that not everyone you hire will work out and that sometimes you need to let some go. After you have worked up the courage to confront the issue and finally taken the hard decision to fire someone you usually get a very positive reaction from their co-workers. In fact, the usual comment is - 'Why did you wait so long?' Almost without exception, the co-workers have recognized that the individual was not pulling their weight, undermining the group culture and productivity and a millstone on everyone.

The lesson is always to recognize when you have it wrong and act quickly. Your employees will usually thank you for doing so. On the other side of the coin, take your time before you add a new employee. Too often we hire without checking the references properly or don't ensure that the individual will fit into the culture of the organization. Also recognize that a new employee adds costs to the organization and you need to be confident you have the business to support them even when the going gets tough.

7. *Create Deep Expertise*

Too often we think of competitive advantage as just being formal Intellectual Property (IP) such as patents, brands, trademarks, licenses etc. But, in fact, one of the best and most enduring sustainable competitive advantages is a deep expertise in a niche market problem.

There are numerous advantages of deep expertise. It takes a long time to develop and operationalise which means that a new entrant to your sector has a long hard road to go before they catch up with you. You develop economies of scale and learning curve effects which makes your operations more cost effective and more productive. You engage with customers in their own language which earns you respect and reduces their perceived risk of working with you. Your competitive advantage through deep expertise will reduce your sales cycles, improve your margins, reduce your competition and create more resilience in your business through repeat sales and referrals.

8. *Someone Has To Be The Boss*

At the end of the day a business is not a democracy and someone has to be the boss and take the hard decisions. You can't have a situation where the employees don't know who has the last say or where several people say they are in charge. When they disagree you have a dysfunctional business.

Even if you start the business with several others, each with an equal share, the business will only operate effectively if one person is given the task of leader. There are simply too many times when there is no right answer and someone has to make a judgement call in order for the business to have some sense of direction. Pick the person who people respect most for their wisdom, leadership and vision and make it work.

9. Define What Problem You Solve

Ask your typical entrepreneur to describe what problem their business solves and you will get a dump on products, services, features and functions, but you won't find out about what problem they solve. Entrepreneurs are especially bad at describing the need they fill or the problem they solve. They also can't tell you who their ideal customer is.

If the business cannot clearly articulate what need they address or problem they solve, what will they be setting out in their marketing collateral and what will their sales staff be saying to prospective customers. If we can't say what we do and who we do it for - why would we assume that those with the need we address will be able to find us so they can buy from us?

Ask your current customers what need or problem you addressed for them and check this against your own marketing literature to see if you have a disconnect. Getting this right is fundamental to effective marketing.

10. Stick To What You Know Best

Failure rates for startup ventures is quite high - generally estimated to be about 50% in the first 6 years of the venture. That being the case, the more you can do to improve your probability of success, the greater the chance of survival. What is obvious from observing many businesses over several decades is that it usually takes a new business about 5 years of operations before they really become effective in a new sector. It simply takes a long time to understand how a marketplace works, to know where the risks are and how to manage them and to build a network of contacts within the sector.

What is obvious from this insight is that you can gain a considerable advantage by developing a business in a sector in which you already have considerable experience. If you already have the connections, know how business is done and have existing relationships with potential customers and suppliers, your risk exposure is considerably reduced. We should never underestimate what we don't know about a sector and we should, at the same time, acknowledge the advantages we have from our prior experience.

11. Chase The Money

Money in your bank is worth a lot more to you than in the hands of your customer who is neglecting to pay you on time. What we know from hard earned experience is that 'the longer it takes the customer to pay, the more likely they are to default'. Basically, you never stop collecting and you should be insistent that the payment is made on time. Even if they can't pay everything on time, you should ask for partial payment.

However, make sure you have right on your side when you insist on payment. Ensure you have delivered what you said you would and that it is of merchantable quality and fit for purpose. It is very hard to push for payment when you are in the wrong. Get the invoices out quickly and request confirmation of payment. Ask again just before payment date and keep asking frequently thereafter. There is a lot to be said for taking care of the squeaky wheel.

You have to be paid to pay others. You owe it to yourself, your staff and suppliers to do the right thing by them and pay them on time.

12. Obtain The Best Advice

There are many risks to manage in a business and the last thing you can afford is to be exposed because you failed to address a problem correctly or to ensure you had adequate protection in an agreement. Basically, if you pay peanuts for advice you will get monkeys doing the work for you.

The difference between smart advisors and very ordinary ones is not just a few percentage points, it is counted in multiples. Really smart people pay for themselves over and over again. It is worth taking the time to track them down and ask them to do work for you. You can tell the difference immediately. They ask different questions. Their questions are insightful, penetrating, challenging and often uncomfortable as they expose your own lack of preparation. They think about your business first and the problem you are trying to solve rather than giving you an off the shelf solution. Whatever extra they might cost is recouped many times over in the difference they make to your business.

13. Create Interesting And Challenging Jobs

Good people are hard to find and even harder to keep. They usually have no trouble getting a new job and securing the remuneration they want. However, they are not always just motivated by salary, although it is important to pay the market rate. What they often want are interesting things to do and assignments which challenge them.

We neglect at our peril the aspirations of our staff to better themselves or to create for themselves an environment where they enjoy coming to work. While we don't have to create a 100% interesting and challenging environment, we need to have some portion of the job in this mode. People who are challenged and enjoy the work are more productive, more contented with their situation and tend to mix better with other employees. They tend to stay longer, are less demanding in their conditions and are easier to work with.

14. Use Innovation To Compete

To be successful in a sector you need to have some degree of competitive advantage. This doesn't have to be across the whole sector but it should at least provide an advantage in the niche you target. However, just having a competitive advantage is not sufficient to drive continuing profitability or growth. For that you need to create a sustainable competitive advantage. Even formal IP such as patents expire so you can't sit back and rely on any form of competitive advantage over time.

Basically you need to create a culture, process or strategy which continually updates your competitive advantage over time. The answer lies in developing an innovation capability. Whether it is incremental innovation or radical innovation, the only certainty you have of survival, profitability and success is to ensure that your innovative capability continually updates your competitive position. Don't wait until you are desperate to reclaim territory, take the initiative and ensure you stay in front. Innovation is the only sure way to do that.

15. Be Accountable To A Board

It is very easy in business when you are the founder, president or owner to become complacent and make decisions on the fly because you can and not bother to explain or justify your decisions - because you have the authority to do what you like. Big mistake! We all need the discipline of explaining what we are doing and why to someone. It is important to have a reason to think things through carefully, consider all options and control the knee jerk reactions. Being accountable for your decisions and actions, even when you don't have to be, is a very worthwhile discipline to develop in business.

If you can't explain why you are doing something to an intelligent and industry knowledgeable individual, you should take a step back and rethink your decision. Whether you have a formal Board of Directors or an informal coach, the discipline of thinking through the decision and how you will present it to gain approval and support is a very useful mode of operating. Consider, if it is the right decision you should gain support from them. If you can't convince your Board or your coach, are you really sure you are making the right decision? At the end of the day, it may well be your judgement call, but it is worth gaining the feedback to ensure you have thought it through carefully.

16. Reward Exceptional Performance

The way in which you reward and sanction behavior in your business will determine the way in which staff act. You motivate them according to what you encourage and discourage. If you want exceptional performance, you have to show by your actions that you value that form of behavior.

Individuals who contribute to the health, profitability and resilience of the business through their decisions, actions and behavior are worth keeping and certainly worth recognizing in some way. Whether that recognition is 'employee of the month', or a mention in the company newsletter or a special 'thank-you' from the president, it is worth doing. However, don't neglect financial rewards for exceptional contributions or time off or a paid vacation. Perhaps even ask them what would work for them - it might be an education allowance, an opportunity to work on a special project or the chance to go to an industry conference.

Your actions will convey to others in the firm the type of behavior and contribution which the firm values. By rewarding exceptional performance you will encourage others to make the effort.

17. Set The Right Customer Expectations

While it might feel good to 'exceed the customer's expectation', it is usually the worst thing you can do. Meeting the customer's expectation on the other hand is the smartest thing you can do. So why not exceed it? The problem is that you end up resetting the expectation so that next time you have to step up to the better performance. If you cannot consistently meet the higher level of performance, you end up with a dissatisfied customer.

Customer satisfaction is directly related to expectation. A customer who receives what they expected time and again will be satisfied. The worst thing that can happen in a customer experience is to have some form of random result, whether good or bad. The they don't know what to expect, they may prefer to buy elsewhere. If you want repeat sales and referrals, the best thing you can do for your business is to ensure your marketing communications specify exactly what you do and then ensure you deliver against that outcome every time.

18. Plan For The Worst Case

Every entrepreneur I have talked to has told me stories of things which have gone wrong. Missed deadlines, cancelled orders, payments not being received, employees leaving at critical times, people getting ill, new competitors and so on. Even a great business won't be immune to problems and those that are not planned for can do real damage to the business. What you need to do is to test out various scenarios to ensure you know what decisions you would make in the event of a serious problem.

Once we understand the worst case, we can put in place strategies to cope, mitigate, avoid or respond. It is not that this becomes the business plan, we should still plan for what we realistically expect, but we should have fallback strategies in case things go wrong. In preparation, we might arrange additional funding sources, cross train staff, plan for succession, have back up plans for generating income, plan to delay discretionary expenses and so on. Understanding where the risks are and what tactics can be employed is the smart way to cope with future problems.

19. Keep The Bank Informed

Banks are not in the risk business. The margin they have between the rate of interest they pay on deposits and what they charge on lending is often as low as 2%. It takes a lot of banking business to recover from a bad debt. That being the case, you can't expect them to support you if they don't know what is happening in your business and they have no basis on which to make a judgement about your ability to manage through a dip in revenue. They are not your friend and they are not a shareholder in your business but they are a supplier and an essential one at that.

Banks will react quickly if they think their money is at risk. They have been known to seize money in accounts just at the time you are about to pay payroll or your suppliers. Basically, if you don't keep them up to date and provide them with a view of your future business, you can't blame them for overreacting. They need to build up a knowledge of your business and of the manner in which you tackle problems. The earlier you can inform them of a problem situation and show them how you will manage through, the greater the chances you will have their support. They also do not want to meet you when you have an immediate problem. You need to update them on a regular basis on the business and show you can manage good times and bad.

20. To Control You Have To Measure

If you don't know what to expect or if you have no targets to measure performance against, you will simple be in reactive mode. At the same time, if you don't measure activity or performance, you have no way of knowing whether the activity is good, bad or indifferent. You can't take corrective action if you don't know what good or bad performance is.

Don't be misled by your financial reports. They are usually well out of date and only measure a very limited set of activities within the firm. They are normally at a high level of aggregation and therefore tell you little about what is happening operationally. What you really need to do is to identify the critical activities in the business, set performance targets and then put in place monitoring of the activity as close as you can to when the activity takes place. By monitoring activity levels, you can quickly determine what is a realistic level of performance and then you have the basis for taking action in the case of a variation. It is just as important to know when you have superior performance. We can learn a lot from what we are doing well and use this knowledge to improve the business.

Without measuring activity we cannot set performance targets, make people accountable or reward good performance and sanction poor performance. Measurement is the basis of management control.

21. Educate And Cross Train Workers

Specialization and dedication is highly productive but it can also be boring for staff. Feeling stuck in a job without hope of enhancing your career or improving future employment prospects is demotivating for employees. At the same time, allowing an individual to dominate a job puts the firm at risk if the person suddenly leaves or is away ill.

What I found over many years of employing staff is that they welcomed the opportunity to learn new skills, participate in new activities and educate themselves to improve their prospects. Instead of losing staff, I ended up retaining them longer than the average in the industry. When the business went though difficult times, instead of staff leaving to find better security, they were prepared to stay because their wider range of skills and better education made them recognize they were highly employable and didn't need to worry about getting a job if they were suddenly made redundant. The cross training and education opportunities also made them appreciate their current position and made them more interesting and contented staff.

22. Ask Your Customers For Feedback

By buying from your firm, your customers have actually given you a vote of confidence and have made an investment in your reputation and future. They want you to be successful and want to be proud of the fact they chose you as a supplier. While this may feel trite, many customers actually do feel this way and are more than happy to give you feedback on your products and services to make you more successful. We only need to ask them.

Your customers usually have greater experience of your products and services than you do, after all, you are only the manufacturer or provider. They actually are the users and consumers. So in many ways, they understand what the products should do or what the service should provide. They can tell you what works and what doesn't, what can be improved, how the service or products can be adapted or enhanced to provide a better solution and so on. Many have experience of competitor products and services and are often willing to provide you with competitor information. Whether you use a survey, telemarketing or gather them together for a panel session, many will provide you with information which you will find invaluable in improving your business.

23. Build Recurring Revenue

The first objective of any business is to survive so strategies which improve business resilience have to be high on the agenda. We only get to do the interesting things in our business if we last long enough to have the time and resources to do them.

One of the most successful strategies to create resilience is to build up the level of recurring revenue in the business. By recurring revenue I mean revenue which the firm can rely on even in an economic downturn. You should review how you can implement long term customer agreements, loyalty schemes, customer engagement activities, customer entanglement strategies and on. Develop products and services which sell back into the existing customer base such as maintenance, auditing, training, accessories, upgrades and so on. You need to create reasons why your customers need to come back for additional products or services.

Creating good customer experiences can also improve the resilience of the business if it results in repeat sales or a high level of referrals. A healthy business might aim to have 50% of its business from its current customers. This provides a solid buffer for economic downturns or new competitors entering the sector.

24. Engage Your Customers

Your current customers who are actively using your products or services are familiar with what you do and are on your radar, but what of the prior customers - what are you doing for them? We know from experience that it is easier to sell more products and services to existing and prior customer than to chase down new ones. If we neglect prior customers we give up huge opportunities to resell or to encourage them to give referrals. Where we can, we should be finding ways to stay in touch and engage with them to keep us in their sights.

Think of all the ways in which you can engage customers - newsletters, product updates, product releases, charity events, sponsorship, customer surveys, special offers and so on. The list is endless if you use some imagination. What you want is for them to remember the good experience they had with your products and services and to quickly recall your name when they have a similar need or someone they know asks for a referral.

Not all customers will buy again but they all have opportunities to refer you to someone with a problem you can solve. You want to be the one recommended.

25. Develop Strong Values

The most effective way to run a larger business is for every person in the business to be able to predict what the right strategy is when faced with a situation or problem. Not that you want everyone making decisions necessarily, but the fact that they all understand how the business will react and what decision is likely to be made adds a degree of stability and predictability to the business. That is good for morale as well as making it easier to manage the business.

We should not underestimate the micro decisions which employees make every day. Whether they are advising a customer on a service delivery or working on a project, they are all making decisions. What you want is a consistent approach to these interactions and decisions. That can only happen if the values underpinning the business are understood, agreed and widely implemented. You can then have confidence that the right decisions are being made across the business.

26. Use Complaints As Feedback

Not only is it nice to know what your customers think, it is actually critical to the health of the business and to its future prospects. Complaints are one of the best feedback systems you have. They are independent of the business and if not filtered out, can provide you with what is happening at the coal face of your business. They let you know if your products are doing what they are meant to do, whether your services are providing value for money and whether all your operational systems are doing what they are supposed to do. In other words, you are getting a free audit.

While it would be nice to have no complaints and to stop problems before they occur, you really do want the earliest possible feedback on whether the business is operating properly. Complaints need to be given serious attention and the activity given authority to take action to investigate and compensate. A complaint handed well results in a satisfied customer. A complaint you never hear or which is badly handled is an angry customer who will undermine your business.

27. Productize Knowledge

One of the major contributors to high growth is the principle of scalability. Higher scalability or replication occurs when products are standardised, simplified and packaged so that a larger number of people can sell, install and use them. The problem with knowledge in peoples' heads it that it is very difficult to scale thus it severely limits the growth of the firm. In order to grow, a lot of people have to be recruited and then trained on the knowledge. If, however, that knowledge can be embedded into a product, the ability to more quickly deploy it increases dramatically.

The manner of productizing can vary but in essence it means taking knowledge and putting it into a form which can be deployed more quickly in a standardized form, that might mean a documented process, a software product such as a diagnostic or a tangible product such as a control system. Once productized, the product is standardised so that training is easier and more routinized. Less knowledgeable people can be used for its deployment and standard methods can be utilized in the selling process. Rapid growth depends on the ability to scale. Without productizing the knowledge, growth is inhibited.

28. If Its Not Fun – Get Out

Being in an early stage company is challenging at the best of times. Almost without exception, you will be dealing with a lack of finance, a shortage of resources, more things you need to do than you can cope with, people who don't have the same level of passion for the venture as you and friends and relatives who think you have lost your mind to do what you are trying to do. You have to have great fortitude, doggedness, persistence and absolute faith that you will succeed. If it all gets too hard, if you lose the faith and you wonder whether you can go on, then you need to let go and sell out.

Business isn't always fun but it should be exciting, energizing and engaging. It is what gets you up in the morning and the last thing you think of before you nod off to sleep. It consumes your day, dominates your conversation and keeps you alert. It is the fire in your belly. If that stops, it is hard to reignite the flame. All too often when we feel we are drowning and can see no way out, it is quite possible there is no way out. There are times when you should get out. Better to let go, regroup and come back reinvigorated with a new idea and start again.

There are no guarantees in entrepreneurship, but we know that we all have more than one venture in us. We just hope the first one and the last one are successful.

29. Don't Compromise On Ethics

There will be times when you have to make tough decisions and there will be times when there is nothing to guide you but your personal values. The nature of ethics suggests that, when the going gets hard and you have to make the tough decision, can you live with your decision? Whenever you compromise your basic beliefs, you have to live with the consequences and the nagging thought that, just perhaps, there was another decision you should have made.

A great test of the right decision is whether you can stand up in a public forum and justify your decision. We can only do that if we have strong fundamental beliefs which we stick to. The question of what is right is often different for each of us. It comes from our upbringing, our parents, schooling and religious and cultural beliefs. This is why different people will make a different decision given the same set of facts. What is important is that you know what you would do and others around you share those ethical beliefs so that you stand together in the face of a difficult decision. When you compromise those beliefs, you start to undermine your moral authority but also your own self belief in what you are doing. Stick to your beliefs.

30. Find The Compelling Need

What really drives venture growth? This is a question which has plagued academics, entrepreneurs and policy makers for generations. It was my own experience across several ventures which finally gave me the insight into the critical drivers of growth. What became very obvious was that the most critical element of all was a principle called the 'compelling need'. This represent the degree to which the problem or need the business is solving is critical to their target customer. Basically, is this something they have to have or is it a nice to have?

Compelling needs include products which save lives, prevent or reduce severe physical or mental pain or keep people out of jail. While this is the gold standard, we need to seek out those problems which have a degree of urgency for the buyer. When the buyer can choose not to buy or to delay or substitute another product, our power to entice the buyer is substantially weakened.

Solving a compelling need is the most critical of all aspects of business resilience, growth and profitability.

31. Build Teams Not Islands

In any business it is very easy for individuals and entire departments to become isolated and detached from the rest often with their own agenda. When this happens, the fabric of the business is rendered in pieces and the chances of a coordinated response to an opportunity or problem severely inhibited. We need to think of the business like an automobile where every part has a function to play and where the whole is much better operationally than the parts. We need to work to ensure that everyone is part of the team and not just an on-looker.

The role of the entrepreneur is both leader and visionary. They need to create an environment where everyone looks forward to the rewards which come from their combined success. The reward for success can be as simple as achieving industry recognition or having done something outstanding. But without something which pulls everyone together around a common purpose, it is very easy for individuals and departments to focus on their own goals, often at the expense of others.

32. Use Deal Makers Not Deal Breakers

Lawyers are trained in advocacy, that is, they will fight tooth and nail to advance your cause and protect you at all costs. Regrettably, this often tends to go beyond what is reasonable to the other side and you end up in drawn out negotiations as each party digs in to protect their turf. The better lawyers start with the business outcome you wish to achieve and tell you what is reasonable and what share of the risks you need to take for there to be a fair and equitable deal.

I have seen both deal makers and deal breakers at work and the difference is staggering. Instead of deals polarizing people, the deal maker brings people together around common goals, shows where each party should make concessions and introduces protections for the other side which they should be requesting. Both sides come to respect the quality of the advice and the deal gets done quicker and usually, with lower legal fees. Lawyers who won't give an inch, while they are protecting their client from every possible risk, often cause the deal to go bad. You often end up with no deal at all even if you were willing to concede some issues.

33. Make Everyone Accountable

Business goes more smoothly when everyone knows what their job is, what they are expected to do and what targets they are to meet. With this in place, you can then hold each person accountable for their own performance. Without this metric, you are letting people off taking responsibility for their own actions.

The advantage of assigning responsibility and thus accountability all the way through the business is that you have certainty as to where decisions are supposed to be made. The person responsible has to collect whatever information they need to make a reasoned decision and be prepared to defend the decision they make. They can't blame someone else if it goes wrong. This structure also gives you the best chance of gathering planning information at a very detailed level. The same person should have the best data or best judgement on what will be the results of their actions in the forthcoming planning periods. Whether it is sending out invoices, making deliveries or making sales, the individual responsible is the best person to suggest how to improve their activity and to predict their results.

34. Develop Strategic Partners

There is an old expression about 'using other people's money' to achieve your objectives. In business, a similar expression could be to 'use other firm's resources' to achieve your business objectives. This is how it basically works when it comes to strategic partners. Basically, we are seeking to achieve is a situation where we work with other businesses to achieve goals which individually would be impossible or more difficult. Alternatively, we work together so that the parties can achieve common goals more easily.

Many companies are able to help you with access to knowledge, marketing resources, their customers, suppliers and advisors with little cost to them but significant benefit to you. At the same time, you may be able to offer them solutions, products or services which make their own businesses more effective. These partnerships can be very effective in joint bidding, marketing campaigns, research and development, joint training and so on. The most likely strategic partners are the ones which have complementary products, sell to the same or similar customers or are dealing with similar technology issues where working together makes sense for both parties.

35. Cash Is King

Every successful entrepreneur I have ever met says that the first priority in business is to manage the cash. The reason is simple. This is the major cause of business failure. You can be very profitable and still go into insolvency if you do not have enough cash to pay your debts and expenses. So managing the cash flow is critical to survival and health of the business.

Many businessman make the mistake of thinking that managing cash is about reviewing business accounts and seeing where the cash is being used. While this is a worthy exercise, the real benefits lie in forecasting the sources and uses of cash. You need to know where and when the cash is coming in and where and when the cash is being applied for an extended period of time into the future. This might be daily, weekly or monthly depending on the sensitivity of the business to forecast errors. It is worth developing a sensitivity analysis around forecast cash flows so that you can see the impact of different assumptions of business activity. Without an accurate forward cash flow it is impossible to properly mitigate risks when cash balances decline or are predicted to go negative. With inadequate planning in this area, the business is likely to fail.

36. Set Realistic Targets

I once participated in a senior executive meeting where the various divisions were told what their targets were without any reference to what they could achieve. They were then told to go away and revise their budgets to meet the imposed targets. Leaving the room, I overheard several state that they would submit the new budgets but simply ignore them and do what they had earlier planned to do under the budgets they had originally submitted. The likely outcome of such a process would be that the targets in most divisions would not be achieved. However, parts of the business which were relying on other sections meeting their targets would then over commit resources. The end result would be a staggering waste of resources, a failure to meet budget and a completely unbalanced business.

The core purpose of the business planning process is to ensure that the sum of the parts adds up to the whole. By bringing everything together we can see how each part interacts with each other, where the interdependencies occur and what the drivers of the business are. By ensuring that we have reasonable and achievable targets for each part of the business, we have the greatest chance of ensuring that we have a smoothly working business where no one part is out of kilter with the rest. No point in marketing having an aggressive campaign if we can't deliver product and no point in manufacturing product if there is no one to sell it. Getting commitment from the bottom up and then fine tuning the allocation of resources to achieve the overall goals is a critical planning process but it is severely undermined without commitment at all levels.

37. Lock In Customers

Where you can, you should create a situation where your customers willingly give up their rights to engage with your competitors. You might find this a bit confronting but in fact, we as individuals willingly enter into agreements all the time where we commit for extended periods of time to one supplier. Think of your mobile phone, mortgage, life insurance, car lease, internet service and office rental agreements. There are penalties for early termination but also, usually, concessions or benefits for signing up long term.

We can often create some form of 'lock in' in our customer agreements. These can be preferred supplier agreements, maintenance and service agreements, cumulative rebates or discounts, joint ventures or strategic partnerships. The objective is to engage with the customer on a longer term basis and to entangle the customer with your business so that there are disincentives for them to terminate the agreement or change suppliers. Customers are usually reluctant to switch suppliers if there is a 'switching cost' associated with moving suppliers. This might be the risk of making the wrong decision or simply the delays, costs, hassles and stress of moving. Our task must always be to make it easier to deal with us than to switch.

38. Document Your Processes

One of the major problems of selling services is that the customer can't see and touch what they are about to buy. They often see the purchase as an act of faith. Because of this, their perceived risk is usually quite high. What we need to do as the vendor is to find ways in which we can provide greater certainty about what is being sold. We need to provide greater clarity and certainty around the outcomes which will come from the purchase and work to substantially reduce the perceived risk.

We can achieve a lot through documented case studies and testimonials. If I can see or hear the outcomes which other customers have achieved, I can have a greater degree of confidence about what I am about to commit to. However, many intangibles are highly customized during the delivery process and so the precise outcome is not known at the outset. In this situation, the process which is used to deliver the service is critical. A well documented process which allows the customer to see how you will undertake the activity can often allay their concerns. This is especially effective if the process is broken down into stages with each stage having its own planning and review components. Instead of seeing a long term commitment with uncertain outcomes, the customer can see incremental outcomes over which they have some influence.

39. Plan For Succession

Businesses put themselves at considerable risk if they don't plan for the temporary or permanent absence of critical staff. While we can plan for those absences which are scheduled, such as vacations or business travel, we can't plan for someone being sick for an extended period or someone suddenly resigning. These latter situations can have a devastating impact on the firm if nothing has been done to ensure you have a succession plan.

Temporary staff can sometimes be used to cover a sudden absence or departure but this is often suboptimal as the absent person often has a lot of business intelligence. The only effective way to cope with these situations is to have a succession plan which anticipates an absence for an extended period of time. Individuals can be cross trained, work together on projects or have access to personal files when an absence occurs. Each person can be asked to create a succession plan so that the information needed to undertake their job in the event of an extended absence is well documented. What you can't afford is an extended disruption because you failed to put a succession plan in place.

40. Admit Mistakes and Fix Them

For over 3 years I worked for an acquirer where the senior executives were unwilling to ever admit a mistake to a customer even when it was glaringly obvious that the company was at fault. They would find every excuse they could to avoid responsibility and usually blamed the customer. When my business was originally acquired we had a 98% customer satisfaction level. When I left three years later, the customer satisfaction level was about 5%. The company eventually got into severe financial difficulties and was bought for a fraction of its prior worth.

Clearly customers know when you are at fault. Denying it simply makes the situation much worse and ends up creating a really bad reputation in the marketplace. Those companies who immediately admit fault, do all they can to rectify the problem and go out of their way to compensate the customer usually have outstanding customer satisfaction levels. These are also the companies who have high repeat sales and very high referrals.

41. Reward Having A Go

What distinguishes entrepreneurial cultures is that they chase opportunities. I am not suggesting that they don't subject them to rigorous analysis but opportunities are by their very nature risky, so some are destined to fail. If you want your staff to be motivated to consider the opportunities, submit them for evaluation and then actively participate in doing something about them, you have to allow some to fail. When that happens, the people who participated can't be blamed or passed over. The fact that they were willing to step up and have a go should itself be recognized and rewarded.

Command and control cultures stifle creativity and innovation. This is the last outcome you need as an entrepreneurial firm. What you want is lots of ideas coming forward, no matter how bizarre they might seem. Subject them to the usual opportunity evaluation tests but be proactive. It is only by having a go that the successful ones will survive and contribute to your business. Competitive advantage is substantially based on innovation, so the more ideas you start with the greater the chance of finding some that work. Make sure you reward those who participate whether their idea is successful or not.

42. Develop An Exit Plan

Why do we do what we do? Good question and different entrepreneurs will have different reasons for the here and now. But what of the end game? What do you want to achieve long term? For most entrepreneurs it is cashing up - being rewarded for many years of hard work and taking the risk and shouldering the responsibility for the wellbeing of their employees. If an exit is on your horizon then consider this - there is a reasonable chance you will be made an offer for your business. Are you ready for that discussion?

Of course, we should never forget that we are in the risk business. What happens if we get into a situation where the business will not survive. How quickly can you put the business up for sale? Can you attract the best offers? The last business I had, we were heading into insolvency but we managed to sell the business to Peoplesoft in two weeks for six times revenue. You can only do that type of deal if you are well prepared.

43. Have An Escalation Process

One of the worst thing that can happen in business is for a very disgruntled customer to bad mouth you because you failed to recognize a problem and/or do something about it when it was brought to your attention. Reputations are partly built on good products and services but they are greatly enhanced if you deal with problems, mistakes and errors quickly, efficiently and with generosity.

What I learnt in business is that not everyone has the same generous attitude to the angry or complaining customer. They would rather forget them than deal with the problem. But from a business perspective, these issues are critical and deserve a rapid response. What I did was implement an escalation process where a problem not dealt with in a defined timescale was sent to the next highest level in the firm. This continued until it hit my desk. It did not matter that the problem was being dealt with. What really counted was that the customer saw the level of attention which was being given. Customers loved it.

44. Find Unmet Needs

Far too often entrepreneurs chase the obvious. This simply puts them in the way of competitors. If they do little to differentiate themselves, they are forced to compete on price, reducing their margins and putting their firms at risk. What they should be seeking out are the problems which have not been adequately addressed, trends where demand is moving ahead of supply and niche markets which are not attractive to the large corporations.

Sometimes all it takes is a survey of your current customers. What more can we do for you? What problems do you have where the solution is inadequate? What features and functions can we add which will make your life easier? It doesn't take a lot to find unmet needs. These are especially attractive if they add value to existing customers, introduce cross selling opportunities or provide solutions which open doors quicker and reduce timescales. The good thing about doing something a little differently is that you do not have the same price pressure. You can afford to make a few mistakes and you end up creating additional competitive advantage for yourself.

45. Measure Activity Against Targets

There is a very good reason why we have budgets, performance targets, activity level targets and milestones. We need the discipline these bring to the planning functions. Of course they also need to be coupled with responsibility and accountability. But the discipline of setting and agreeing targets confronts people with the need to work out how they are going to meet the targets. In doing so, the firm gets a reality check on whether the targets can be met. It also ensures that resources are marshalled to the right places and are not frittered away or wasted on things which don't add value to our corporate objectives.

Of course targets without systems to periodically measure performance are simply useless. The whole concept of performance management is to have both targets and performance measurement, followed by a review, explanations for deviations, corrective action and lessons learned. Because so much of the operations of the firm are inter-woven and interdependent with other aspects of the firm, ensuring that all targets are mutually dependent is critical.

46. Exclude Personal Expenses

It is very tempting to see your business as a personal piggy bank which can bankroll your personal expenses, especially entertainment and travel. But this is one of the worst mistakes entrepreneurs make. One day you will want to bring in a partner or investor or sell the business. When that happens, the due diligence takes the business apart and runs a magnifying glass over everything. The entrepreneur who runs a clean company, who can justify, from a business perspective, everything which has been expensed through the business will be the winner.

What happens when the due diligence turns up personal expenses is that the investor or trade sale buyer doesn't know how far the abuse extends. This means a much greater depth audit just to uncover the depth of the problem. Then of course you have the concern as to whether this practice will continue if you are the potential partner or investor. In the end it undermines the confidence which the partner, investor or trade sale buyer has in the firm. On the other hand, a business which demonstrates a clear demarcation between the expenses of the business and the personal expenses of the entrepreneur and staff, shows a high ethical and professional position which often permeates through everything else the firm does. A very good position to be in.

47. Install a Good Reporting System

We should never underestimate the power of a comprehensive management reporting system, even in the smallest of firms. It is very hard for any entrepreneur to understand everything which is going on in a firm and it is certainly difficult to see trends from close to the action. Sometimes you need to take a step back and have a set of objective reports which can report every aspect of the business in current operational terms but also relative to similar past periods and agreed targets.

I prefer a set of management reports which cover all aspects of the firm's operations. On a daily basis you want to see activity figures. On a weekly basis, look at operational information such as sales, creditors, debtors and weekly activity, especially relative to targets. Monthly data is normally aggregated into financial reports, usually reported as both actual and against a budget. You should ensure that major risk areas are reported on at least once a year, such as succession planning, insurance coverage, recruitment, training and so on. Managing is much more effective if it is supported by a comprehensive set of reports.

48. Pragmatic Beats Perfection

One of the biggest lessons I learned in business was that you have to have something to sell if you are to survive. What this means in practice is that you often release basic products without all the bells and whistles. Getting a product out the door is far more important than producing the perfect product. Inventors, on the other hand, want the perfect product and will fight tooth and nail to add the extra bits of functionality. This tussle between inventor and entrepreneur is a constant battle which goes on in entrepreneurial firms.

What you learn over time is that you can always add the extra features in later versions. What is critical is to get the first product into the market to begin establishing market presence and hopefully, a leadership position. As others come into the market to copy you, the added features of your new releases keep you in the leadership position. You need to take a very hard position with R&D to ensure there is a cutoff for any version release. Basically, you draw a line which says 'that is enough', don't add anything more, leave it alone, get it out. This is very hard for the perfectionists to accept as they can always see how a product can be improved. You have to hold the line if you are to survive and prosper.

49. Focus, Focus, Focus

In the early days of a new firm, survival has to be the primary objective. Unfortunately, because funds are always tight it generally means that you take on anything which will pay expenses, usually compromising the long term objectives of the firm. But once you are past that point and you have enough business to choose what you do, the primary objective must be to tighten the focus of the firm so that you do one thing really well. What that means is, don't solve lots of different problems for different types of customers. Instead, choose what you can do really well for one set of customers and dig deep.

Competitive advantage lies in being better at one thing than your competitors. The more you specialize, the more likely you are to develop the expertise, products and services which will give you that advantage. Focus builds on the advantages which come from learning curve effects and economies of scale. Focus improves your probability of repeat sales and referrals, both essential ingredients for high growth execution.

50. Shotgun Marketing Is A Waste

We need to start our marketing strategy with what problem we solve and who has the problem. We need to know who our ideal customer is and how we can get our message in front of them. So rather than blast our message out to all and sundry, which is effectively the shotgun approach to marketing, we should be using a rifle to zero in on our target customer. Instead of advertising we might be better off with telesales. Instead of putting up an exhibition stand, we might be better running seminars for invited audiences.

What we have to work out is the cost of customer acquisition. Anything we do which puts our marketing resources in front of the wrong prospect is money wasted. We need to design our marketing programs so they focus on where our targets customers can be found. Do they read a specific magazine, attend certain trade conferences, buy from specific retail outlets, belong to certain clubs or use specific credit cards? We need to go where they are and where we get the biggest bang for our buck.

51. Lowest Price Is Fragile Positioning

In every marketplace there are going to be a range of products which vary in quality, price and functionality. One position which seems to attract more than its far share of attention is the lowest price. This is often seen to be the largest part of the market and therefore the most attractive for the company which wants to grow. However, lowest price is a hard position to build a sustainable business on.

When you take on the lowest price, you are appealing to a customer group who are primarily interested in price. That is, the features and functions which you believe are the things which excite you about your product and which you believe should attract business are actually not important to the customer. They just want the basic features and functions for the lowest price they can find. In fact, less features and functions would probably appeal to them if they could have a lower price. What this means is a dive to the bottom and the company which can achieve the lowest price wins. However, as soon as a competitor finds a way of pushing their price lower than yours, they will take away your market share leaving you nothing to compete with.

52. Always Pay Market Price

No matter what long term incentives you offer employees, any compromise you make in terms of the remuneration they receive now will be resented. Even if you show them what the rewards for long term success will be if they go the distance and the firm successfully executes on a planned high value exit, this will not be sufficient. While smaller firms generally don't offer the same levels of remuneration and benefits as large firms, it is critical that you offer the going market rate.

What is interesting is that employees will often sacrifice long term gains for short term benefits. Part of the logic behind this is that employees live in a world where they compare what they receive currently with what other people with similar skills and experience receive. If they feel that they are under compensated, they tend to resent it. This gradually eats away at them and they will often push to have their remuneration lifted or will leave the firm for another employer who will pay market rates.

Also never pay more than market rates. What happens is that you end up with people who you are stuck with who won't move on because they cannot find anything else which pays as well. You can also be left with a situation where they are out of step with other employees and then you have resentment from the rest of the employees.

53. Join A Peer Group

I have had the opportunity over the last decade of teaching hundreds of mature age practicing entrepreneurs. During the same period, I have also been invited by various entrepreneurs associations to conduct seminars and workshops for their members. What I have found is that entrepreneurs who keep to themselves or don't have the opportunity of developing an entrepreneur's network feel very isolated. Alternatively, those entrepreneurs who are members of a peer organization or have their own personal network of peers are much more resilient coping with business and personal problems.

We accept as entrepreneurs that we are different from the general population. Our focus 24/7 is our business and we take it with us into our personal lives. What this means is that we never get away from our business problems and they dominate our thoughts and often, our conversations. When we have no one who can understand the issues we are dealing with, we end up stressing and internalizing the problems. Those entrepreneurs who can talk to others who have similar problems or have experienced them in the past allow us to voice our concerns in an environment where we will receive sympathy and support and often wise advice. Those entrepreneurs who belong to peer networks have often told me that it was the best thing they ever did.

54. Try Before They Buy

The biggest obstacle we have in closing a sale is the buyer's perceived risk. If they have used the product or service before, they know what they getting for their money and the perceived risk is very low. But what if they have no prior experience and there is no one they can turn to for advice. Confronted with a complex and expensive product or service, you can imagine their reluctance to hand over their money. The way out of this is to find various ways in which the prospect can try before they buy.

There are lots of techniques which vendors use to allow a trial of a product or service. Products can be made available for trial periods or taken to the home or work location so they can see them in situ. Alternatively, a demonstration might be arranged for an individual or a group. Services are more difficult to trial but sometimes a short or limited experience can demonstrate the quality of the potential outcome. Another method often used is a live simulation undertaken by a member of the firm's staff or a video of the product or service in use. What we have to achieve is to lift the prospect's level of confidence in the outcome they seek. Some form of limited exposure to the actual product or service in use will often overcome their hesitation.

55. Quality Pays

We are often told that 'quality pays' but usually without the explanation of why that is so. A quality product should work as per the specification and it should do so every time it is used. A very simple explanation but it is highly related to customer expectation. What we know is that customer satisfaction relates directly to customer expectation. Customers expect product to work properly. Satisfied customers buy again and tell others how good the product or service is.

On the other hand, poor quality results in products not working correctly. This results in recalls, higher levels of complaints, higher warranty expenses and lower levels of repeat sales and referrals. The benefits of better quality are very obvious if you think of profit margins. When we look at administrative or manufacturing operations, the case is very strong. It is much harder to fix a mistake or problem which has been allowed to stay in a value added process for some time. Rework is both disruptive and expensive. The lowest cost of production and the highest levels of productivity will come from catching errors at the point they occur. A culture which has a zero tolerance for allowing errors and mistakes is one which has a much higher chance of becoming a market leader.

56. Keep Staff Informed

Some firms treat employees like mushrooms - keep them in the dark. Their culture is one where the senior management believes it is dangerous to let lower level employees know what is going on in case the risks in the business are exposed and staff leave. However, this style of management fails to appreciate the higher risk of allowing rumors and misinformation to infect the workplace. Employees are not stupid and they can put isolated bits of information together to create a picture of the health of the business, however, their interpretation of what is happening and how management is dealing with the various issues facing the firm might be wildly wrong.

A more proactive culture informs employees so that everyone has a comprehensive picture of what is happening and an understanding of how the firm is dealing with the pressures it faces. The advantage of this approach is that there are no surprises and individuals who have good ideas can come forward to assist in the strategy. Often people in operational and sales activities will have information which is not readily available to senior management. This information can sometimes throw up insights and ideas to enable the firm to cope with pressures or execute on opportunities. While there are risks, keeping people informed and involved is the better strategy.

57. Leave Your Ego At The Door

Entrepreneurial firms are often very finely tuned. They are usually under pressure due to under resourcing and lack of funding. They exist on a knife edge between success and failure. That being the case, you need everyone in the firm to contribute ideas to its success. A culture which encourages pragmatic solutions, honesty and a willingness to step forward and contribute are essential ingredients of success. The last thing you can afford is for anyone to have a big ego and think they are better than everyone else. You need to avoid situations where any one person feels they have the only solution to a problem and are not open to advice or keep everything to themselves in case others see a weakness or fault with their decision.

My advice has always been to employ people who can go beyond their personal issues and focus on what is the right thing to do for the firm. The last thing you need in business is for someone to make decisions purely on what is good for them at the possible expense of finding the right solution for the firm as a whole. We can only have meaningful conversations if individuals can fully contribute without feeling that others are judging them. Problems need to surface quickly so they don't get to be bigger problems. We need to ensure that, while there may be performance implications for contributing to the creation of the problem, there are serous sanctions for hiding problems.

58. Never Oversell Or Over Promise

One of the worst things which can happen to you in business is to commit to a deal which you know you either can't fulfill or will struggle to fulfill. It may seem great at the time you make the sale, but inevitably it comes back to bite you. If you fail to deliver, you may have to give the money back, write off any work you have completed, manage the reputation damage which stems from the activity and argue with the salesperson to have any sales commission refunded. All very nasty things to deal with.

However, it is the longer term effects which are much more damaging. Apart from a lack of trust by prospective customers and the own goal you scored against your competitors, the internal effects are very damaging. Once your operational staff lose confidence in your rogue salesperson, they will try to avoid working with them, inflate the estimates to give themselves a buffer or quietly let prospects know that they can't trust the salesperson and encourage others to doubt what the salesperson says. You end up with a 'them' and 'us' culture where lack of support and cooperation is the norm. In such a situation, it becomes impossible to operate an effective business.

59. What Will Go Wrong Probably Will

It is probably overly pessimistic to think that what can go wrong will, but even so, it is a great way to manage risk exposure. Basically, if you don't have an approach to planning which considers risks, the chances are that you will be caught short and your business will suffer as a result, perhaps even fail. Our planning process needs to consider the most likely risks and plan for those, that is only prudent. Planning for unusual risks is probably taking it too far but what we do need to do is at least think the worst situations through and see if there are strategies which we could employ which take little effort but keep us on the main course.

We all willingly pay our burglary and fire insurance premiums and yet know the risks of such events are very small, but the loss we incur if they happen is very high. The same logic applies in business, we need to assess the impact of possible delays, threats, accidents and so on, and consider which ones we need to cover for and which we take a risk on. At least by going through the process we go into the future with an understanding of the risks rather than simply ignoring them. In practice, there are many risks which can be covered relatively easily but should be considered in case we miss something which needs attention.

60. Create Value Beyond Functionality

One of the things which I constantly tell entrepreneurs is to think beyond functionality when they are creating customer value. Far too often I hear entrepreneurs talk about products and features and functions as if that is the only thing which the customer is interested in. Yet, when you look around, you find numerous successful companies which have built their reputation around intangible attributes of their customer experience. What differentiates one airline from another when they all use the same planes, use a common ticketing and check in system and serve the same meals?

Customers are interested in every aspect of the sale activity from where they find information, how they evaluate the product, what they feel like when they use it or talk about it and how they interact with your employees during and after the sale. They are also often engaged with you long after the initial sale. Value to the customer can have many dimensions beyond just solving the immediate problem. It is the overall experience which they remember. Your task as a vendor is to create an experience which taps into multiple forms of value not just functionality. By creating a wider set of experiences you can differentiate your business and develop a unique competitive advantage.

61. Find A Business Partner

Being in business is not easy. Many entrepreneurs liken it to a roller coaster ride. That being the case, when you are doing it alone, it is even harder. Many sole entrepreneurs tell me how lonely they feel and how they have to carry the full weight of the business. Few are willing or able to share the worries of the business with their spouses or life partners. They say that the normal ebb and flow of business can seem like a continuous flow of problems and that can look scary to the person who worries about their security, their children's education and where the mortgage payments will come from if the business fails.

What I found works really well for many entrepreneurs is to have one or more partners who work together in the business. This means that there are other people who you can take into your confidence, share the stress and worries about normal business issues but also work together to find solutions for problems. It is so much easier to cope with a problem if there are others who can share the load. Even having the ability to discuss a problem with someone who understands what you are dealing with is a great asset in business. The only thing you have to be very careful about is choosing the right partner.

62. No One Is Indispensable

If you are lucky, you will have some employees who are unbelievably good. They are super productive, get on with everyone and never ask for more than they deserve. Then one day they announce they are leaving; going back to school, moving interstate with their new spouse or off to do charitable work overseas. You are devastated because you know how rare they are.

Then there are the great salespeople who close more than their fair share of deals. However, you discover that they have been putting in false expense claims, over promising on sales or making unacceptable sexual advances to a staff member. You have no choice but to fire them.

In both cases you have lost someone who will be missed because of their outstanding contribution to the business. But the reality is that this will happen over and over again. What is amazing is that the business survives, new people turn up or step up and life returns to normal. What we have to ensure is that we never lock ourselves into one person so much that the business cannot continue without them.

63. *Have Your Business Audited*

Can you really be sure that you have done everything you need to do to meet all your compliance requirements. Can you be sure there are no errors in your systems which are misleading you or that proper authority has been applied to all the expenses. It would be a rare entrepreneur who claimed he knew enough about his business and about the legal obligations to state that he wouldn't benefit from a proper independent inspection by experts.

Apart from making sure the systems are working correctly, the compliance obligations met and any serious errors detected, there is a great deal of comfort to the entrepreneur in having an independent audit. In a way, it is a method of being accountable to yourself. You want to know that you have done the job correctly, you have not overlooked something important and your systems are operating correctly. You also want the advice which comes with the audit on how you could improve your systems. It is important to know that you have your accounting and other governance information up to date if you need a loan or wish to entice an investor into the business. This is something you cannot leave to the last minute.

64. You May Have To Fire Your Friends

You may have started the business as friends and colleagues but the reality of business is that the business cannot have any passengers. Everyone has to contribute and at a level which the market demands of them. If they can't do the job, put in the hours or carry their fair share of the load, they undermine the entire operation.

One of the most difficult decisions an entrepreneur will make is to recognize that their relative or friend is holding back the business and they have to go. Tough as it is, it will be the right decision to enable the business to move forward and prosper. It is a decision between friendship and the business but if you have other employees, there is an obligation to them as well. You cannot really do the right thing by those you have recruited into the business if you compromise the health of the business by continuing to employ people who don't make the grade. If you don't take appropriate action, you are sending a message to all the employees that you are willing to compromise your position and your standards. In the end that will undermine your authority and their faith in you as the leader.

65. Have Customers Sign Off

We all know that cash is king but if you don't have systems to plan and manage it, you haven't really learned the lesson. One of the most difficult things to do is to collect the cash from customers where you have a combination of product and service delivery. Customers will find every possible excuse not to pay or to delay payment. In many ways it is like going into battle. It takes a lot of preparation and very good tactics to ensure you get your money when it is due.

You need to start by setting very clear expectations of what you are providing and the terms of payment. It is critical that you are able to clearly specify the intended outcome of any delivery so that you can verify and document that you have met your obligations. As soon as you can, have the customer sign off on the outcome. This is usually easiest if you do it as soon as you have the evidence you have met your obligations. Do this with staged deliveries as well. Once the customer signs off, send out the invoice and start the process of collection. The customer sign off gives you considerable leverage and takes away the ability of the customer to argue you have not met your obligations as an excuse not to pay.

66. Barter Where You Can

Finding a way of trading resources which you have with resources you need is a really good way of overcoming a shortage of funds. What we should recognize is that many companies have things which they can provide at marginal or not cost to them. On the other hand, you may have services or resources which you can provide for which you will not incur significant outlay. Bartering what you have for what you need makes a lot of sense.

There may be many things which you would like to have but which you cannot afford, or at least afford at that point in time. What if you could obtain additional office space by trading some services or obtain the shared use of a conference room by trading some advice. You need to think about what you have which can contribute to another business which has marginal cost to you but in return, what they could offer you which would be valuable to you but negligible cost to them. You can also trade equity for specialised services. Your lawyer or accountant may be prepared to take a small stake in the firm in return for professional services. Think laterally and you might come up with some interesting arrangements.

67. Don't Forget Your Family

You would be hard put to find any entrepreneur who said that being in business was easy and that it didn't take a toll on their family. The fact is that being in your own business is 24/7. There are no weekends or holidays. The phone can ring at any time, even in the middle of the night and the buck stops with you. This can get very stressful on the rest of the family who feel that they must always take second place. When you don't turn up at school events, miss birthdays and take phone calls during family dinners, you are in serious danger of losing the support of your family.

What we often forget is that family is forever and the business is transient. Few businesses last more than a dozen years. They either go under or we sell the business. That being the case, we need to put the business into perspective and recognize that it is only one part of our life and even then, only a temporary part. We need to set aside time for family and structure the business in a way where we can take weekends and vacations occasionally and spend quality time with the family and let them know they are important. Entrepreneurs have very high divorce rates because they forget to look after this part of their life.

68. Don't Assume – Get The Evidence

All too often we make decisions on our gut feel or instinct and then regret it later. Usually it is because we didn't take a little time to do some checking. Whether it is hiring a new employee, developing a new product, setting a price or opening up a new territory, you should never neglect the facts. There are always relevant facts available if we only bother to take the time to look. We should never accept anything on face value without asking what research went into the decision.

Before you embark on a new project, approve the business plan or commit to new equity, you might ask a few hard questions. What alternatives do we have and what are the outcomes we could achieve under each? Do we need to make the decision now or can we wait while we examine the issue in more depth? What questions should we ask to gain more insights or clarity as to the impact of our decisions? What additional information would allow us to be better informed? What is the evidence we have to enable us to judge the validity of the assumptions underlying our decision? Sometimes the best decision you can make is not to make a decision.

69. Check Your Brand Image

Some firms are clearly in the brand business while others don't think they are, yet we all have brands whether we acknowledge it or not. If you are in business then you are conveying messages in the public domain about your business and your products. Those messages are not just about your product or service features and functions, they are about the intangible characteristics of who you are, what you do and how you do it. They are aspects of quality, integrity, reliability, positioning, availability and so on. Over time they converge around your company name, product labels and even individuals.

Given that you have a brand image whether it was intended or not, it is worth finding out what it is. You need to periodically go into the real world and find out what people think about your business and your products and establish whether your brand image is what you thought it was or, even, what you would like it to be. Start by asking your customers. Then extend your enquiries to your suppliers, service providers and strategic partners. If the people who know you best have a different view of you than the one you are trying to project, you have some work on your hands. Lastly, check with the market you are addressing and find out what they think of you. It can be an enlightening exercise.

70. Acquisitions Are Problematic

If you believe the statistics, acquisitions are the last thing you want to consider. According to countless research studies over several decades, most large scale acquisitions fail to achieve positive shareholder value. Of course, there are many reasons why acquisitions go wrong, but when you see the size of the corporations getting it wrong, you do start to wonder whether you should contemplate doing one yourself.

Generally speaking, the benefits of most acquisitions are to gain the benefits of scale and synergy. But most acquisitions seek to achieve these benefits through integration of people and systems. You could not pick a more difficult path to success. Cultural differences usually cause most integration projects to go wrong and systems always prove far more difficult to integrate than originally anticipated. However, there are other ways to undertake acquisitions. If you steer clear of integration, there are real benefits in leveraging IP across companies, gaining additional capacity from underutilized resources and extending brand benefits to new products.

Before you launch into an acquisition, step back and consider what can go wrong and what impact it will have on your own organization if you fail to realize the acquisition objectives. Often the best path is to grow organically rather than acquire.

71. Beware The Management Fads

We all know that running a business is challenging and we would all like to have that magic bullet which would solve all our problems but beware the newest management fad. If you have been around for a while, you will have seen the next big thing come and go leaving a lot of disappointed entrepreneurs in its wake. Whether it is the secret to selling, recruiting, manufacturing, supply chain management or corporate strategy, there will always be the great breakthrough, usually based on a limited study but great penmanship.

For years now I have been researching the principles of high growth ventures. Almost without exception, I have come back to old and tried fundamentals. Whenever I present on the topic, I have numerous people come to me afterwards and tell me that it is great to be reminded of the basics. Why? Because they make sense. They have wide applicability and they have strong validity over many decades. That is not to say that we don't get useful insights through new techniques and processes but they are never the whole story. We still need a solid business model with good people who can execute on the business strategy.

72. Have An Internal Devil's Advocate

Business is about uncertainties and ambiguities. You can never quite know what is going to happen but at the same time, you can't afford to sit still. Doing nothing might be an option, but it doesn't work for very long. In the end, you have to jump into the unknown, take whatever risks confront you and go for it. However, there is a big danger in jumping too early or not taking the time to consider an issue thoroughly before you commit. When everyone is fully on board, the last thing anyone wants to hear is the doom and gloom person, the nay sayer and the glass half empty person. However, there is a place in every business for a devil's advocate.

When we become overly enthusiastic, we tend to overlook the negatives. We become fixated on the desired outcome and we don't give the negative issues space to be considered. So forcing ourselves to listen to someone who's task it is too pick holes in our logic or to question our assumptions can be a very valuable exercise. Assign someone to the task. Explain that their job is to find as many holes in the business case as possible, to challenge the assumptions, look for alternatives and undermine the proposal. If your business case can survive a determined effort to shoot it down, it will probably work. What you will get out of the exercise is a much stronger and resilient decision.

73. Have A Business Plan

Your business plan will be out of date even before it comes off the printer. You will be lucky if anyone reads it and the most likely outcome is that it will gather dust on a shelf somewhere - so why bother? Even if all this is true (and it probably is), a business plan is one of the most useful documents you will ever produce in an emerging firm. It is most likely the only time when you take the time to look at the whole business as an integrated system. To be effective, the business plan must coordinate every part of the firm. The sales volumes are checked against the inventory levels which in turn are validated with manufacturing and then back into procurement. The operational levels are tested against the employment, recruitment and training numbers and so on.

The reason why venture capital firms want a business plan from you is because they want to see that you understand how every part of the business works and can show how it all works together. They might then dive down into the marketing plan and so on, but they need to see that you understand the implications of changing any part of the plan. The good thing about putting together the business plan is that you have to dig into every part of the business and produce a plan for each part which is integrated into every other part of the business. One of the major benefits is the insight you get into the firm itself. You will uncover problems which need to be fixed and will discover risks which need to be addressed. This is why it is better to write the business plan yourself than have a consultant do it for you. The exercise is well worth the time and effort.

74. Never Trash The Competition

One of the things which I insisted on in my various businesses was that we would never trash the competition. I have seen it happen many times to us and the competitor who engaged in the practice rarely came out of the exercise undamaged. While it may sound attractive, in practice it rarely goes as you expect it to. Perhaps the main reason for not doing it is that prospects actually don't like it. You actually do yourself a disservice in the eyes of the people you are trying to impress.

Where I have seen the exercise go badly wrong is when a salesperson has claimed that a competitor does not have a particular feature in their product. They look really bad when the prospect states that they saw that exact feature the previous day in the competitor's demonstration. Now you are on the back foot and the prospect is having doubts about your own claims. Basically, you can rarely be certain that the competitor hasn't overcome a deficiency or has not announced the feature in their next release. Also, consider that such behavior tends to suggest a lack of faith in your own competitive position. If the only way I can win the business is by running down the competition, I am in trouble.

75. Marketing Is Not Just Advertising

When your marketing department produces a plan which is all about how to spend their budget on advertising, you are in serious trouble. What this says is that they believe marketing is about pushing your way into the market by throwing information at prospects. Not only is this often a complete waste of money but it suggests they don't actually understand the role of marketing. Your marketing department should be planning the strategies for creating great customer experiences not simply creating an advertising message.

When you consider the buyer behavior process, you can see that there are many steps which the buyer will go through even to get to the buying point. How do they identify you as a potential solution to their needs? What information do they have to evaluate your solution? How do you reduce the perceived risk in the purchase? You want marketing to provide strategies to assist you to engage with the customer, improve their customer experience before and after purchase and entice them to buy from you again or to refer you to others. I want my marketing department to tell me how to create great customer experiences not just how to spend money on advertising.

76. *Distributors Have Their Own Agendas*

If your distribution channels include distributors and agents you have a considerable challenge on your hand. What you have to keep in mind is that your success does not necessarily translate into their success. Nor do they necessarily have the same objectives you have. They are independent businesses which have their own objectives, risks and plans and unless you fit into their agendas, your distribution strategy will fail.

For many years I managed our overseas distributor network. I very quickly realized that my success was very dependent on making them successful with my products. I had to work out where they saw risks and work on mitigating those. I needed to understand their objectives so that I could work my own goals into their plans so that when they succeeded I did as well. Basically, I had to construct win-win strategies. I also quickly realized that I could only get serious commitment if they saw I was sharing the risk and putting in the resources and support to make them successful. Once I had the formula right, it worked extremely well.

77. Overseas Takes A Long Time

If there is one thing you learn about doing business overseas it is that everything takes longer than you plan and it always costs many times more than you budget. If you thought doing business in your own country was hard, wait until you try to do it in another one where you don't have the knowledge to fully understand how they do business or what risks you have to deal with. The major problem is that we make lots of assumptions about the way things work. We assume that doing business in a foreign country is really the same as our own except maybe the language is different or they speak the same language with a slight accent. The truth is that almost everything is different and you can't assume anything.

Some reasons are obvious. The legal jurisdiction is different and this influences everything from how you recruit and remunerate staff to how you manage them and make them redundant. There are health and safety differences, pricing, promotion and advertising regulations, banking differences and compliance reporting requirements. But these can be ascertained and planned for. What is harder is to understand the cultural and business norm differences. These can play a big part in your success or failure. Then of course, there are the formal and informal barriers to doing business. Some countries welcome foreign companies and other simply make it difficult to even get started. Without a question it is challenging.

78. Green Is Good

Whether you believe in global warming, organic food or recycling, there can be no question that green is here to stay and that customers generally are in favour of their vendors making an effort to be green. Not that you have to necessarily go overboard and go dark green, but there are basic things you can do which your customers will welcome and be willing to support. It is generally held that an environmental message on a product can justify an additional 5% lift in the retail price, so it being green can often pay for itself.

However, we should not simply consider the obvious marketing message, we also need to consider our own corporate values and what we want to think and say about ourselves. What view do you want your employees to have about their own company? Having a positive view of your place of employment contributes to your self worth. You want your employees to feel good about where they work. So making an effort, whether that is recycling, using low energy lighting or fair trade ingredients or components can make a difference to your internal culture and productivity. Ask your employees what they think about environmental issues and how they could make a contribution. There may be small changes you can make which make people feel good about what they are doing without costing the firm much. Sometimes it actually save money!

79. Make Sure You Can Deliver

Perhaps one of the hardest lessons to learn in business is to not take on a customer commitment where you are not certain you can deliver. When we are small and our primary goal is just to survive, we are very tempted to take anything which comes our way, even if we think it will be a struggle to complete the assignment. However, it is a path to failure. Not only do you regret being caught up in extended time scales, delayed payment and angry customers, it undermines the spirit and energy of your employees, damages your reputation and distracts you from what you should be working on.

You primary operation objective must be to create a competitive advantage in what you do. You need to establish a good set of satisfied customers who will recommend you to others. It is critical to have products and services which are good at what they do and deliver what you promise. There is nothing wrong with taking on something new providing you set the expectation right at the outset. If the customer is willing to share the risk with you, you are still delivering what you say you can. Alpha and beta sites know what they are getting into. They anticipate everything may not go smoothly but they are willing participants. Life is so much easier if you deliver what you promise.

80. Be Ready For The Acquisition Offer

If you are any good at what you do and have something of a profile within your sector, you should anticipate an acquisition offer. There are numerous large firms who grow through acquisitions and they are constantly on the hunt for attractive firms to add value to their business. However, they are usually intolerant of delays in considering their offer and will often walk away from a situation where the firm is unprepared for the conversation. You can miss some great opportunities to cash up if you are not ready for the offer.

You can't plan when an offer might turn up, so you need to be ready. It doesn't take a lot of preparation to have yourself ready for a due diligence investigation or even to have thought through what you would take for the business. But how do you know you have the best offer? The offer may seem attractive and it may be more than you thought you would ever achieve in your lifetime but it still may undervalue your business. The only way you can truly know what you are worth is by having multiple potential acquirers in a competitive bid for the firm. However, with most offers, timing is of the essence. An acquirer is not going to wait while you rush around trying to get some more interested parties, you have to have them lined up at the outset. What that means is you have to be prepared in advance if the offer comes and have a number of potential buyers ready to join the bidding.

81. Wait Until The Money Is In The Bank

The number of times I thought I had a deal closed and signed to not have the cash turn up you could count on more than a few fingers, maybe even several hands. Given that my business was large scale projects, that is quite a lot. What I learned to do was to keep chasing even after the contract was signed. However, if they don't pay you are left fighting in court for the money which is perhaps not a great way to spend your day. So you end up walking away. But the lesson is obvious. Even when you have a signed contract, until the money turns up in the bank, you don't have a deal.

The lesson which follows from this is that you should never spend the money until it is in your bank. Further, be careful how much resource you commit to the customer until you see proof of payment. If they are not paying on time, be careful how long you leave it before holding back on delivery. If you get too far into a project without seeing the money, you may end up writing off whatever you have invested when they don't pay. If they become insolvent, your chances of recovery of your debt may be very slim, especially if you have failed to fully document and have signed off what you have delivered to date.

82. Implement A Zero Tolerance Policy

As the boss you set the limits for behavior. Whatever you tolerate or overlook becomes the boundary line for employee behavior. If you tolerate slackness, then that will be taken advantage of by some staff. If later, you try to tighten up, you will simply meet resistance and resentment. The culture you want to establish needs to be set from the outset. Basically, you need to set a line over which people only cross if they wish to put their employment at risk. Where you have someone who does cross that line, you must as a matter of discipline and policy come down on them hard and in most cases, terminate their employment.

I would apply this policy to cheating, fraud, misappropriation of company resources, misrepresentation, bullying and any form of discrimination or harassment. Apart from the fact that this is good practice, you need to think about the innocent people who are impacted by these actions and the fact that if you don't protect them, maybe no one will. Someone who undermines the goodwill of the business, who creates disharmony or puts the business at risk, in my mind, has no place in the business. It is hard enough in business to keep things going when everything is going well, it is even harder when you have to put up with anti-social or criminal behavior.

83. Set The Example

We have all heard the saying that the culture of an organization comes from its leaders. That is certainly the case in every organization I have belonged to. The values of the leader determine the acceptable culture in the rest of the organization. That being the case, you need to be especially sensitive to what you say and do. Your behavior and decisions will convey meaning to the rest of the organization about what you value and what they need to do if they want to be successful in your organization.

Organizational culture grows over time from the shared experiences of those who work within it. While there may be stated values, the real ones are those which come from practice. The way in which people behave towards each other, what gets rewarded and sanctioned and the stories about what the business has celebrated contribute to its real culture. You need to be very careful in how you recognize achievement, or not, as this conveys what you value. You need to show what you value by how you act yourself and in the decisions you take. What comes from the top permeates to the bottom.

84. Treat Suppliers Fairly

You will recall the old maxim 'treat others as you would have them treat you'. This certainly applies in business and you should apply this to customers and suppliers. In an early stage firm everything is tight. We are always short of cash and often walking a knife edge between boom and bust. That being the case, we need the goodwill of our suppliers when times get tough. But if you want their cooperation when you need it, you have to treat them well during the good times.

Far too many firms treat their suppliers as transactions rather than partners. They seek out the lowest price, push them hard on discounts and then delay payment as long as they can. Basically, they see them as inputs and transactions rather than other firms doing something similar to what they are doing, trying to survive and make a living for their employees. However, if you treat them as partners and with respect, they will work with you through the good times and bad to the extent they are able. It is essential to have them on your side when you need them.

85. Create Good Customer Experiences

High growth firms have a much higher level of repeat sales and referrals than low growth firms. Their marketing costs per transaction are lower and their sales cycles are shorter. They have a reputation for 'going the extra mile' for their customers. Basically, they create good customer experiences which translates into satisfied customers and this in turn results in higher recurring income.

The customer experience is more than just getting the sale, it is creating satisfaction across the entire sale transaction life cycle. This covers need recognition, after sale support and product disposal at the end of its useful life. You want the customer to reflect on their interaction with you and recognize that, in every phase of it, the experience was a positive one. Where many firms fall down is they believe their obligation finishes with the sale and that the customer should be satisfied if the product or service meets the need. But customers don't think that way. They think of the entire experience and this is what you need to target in order to create high growth momentum.

86. Don't Over Borrow

Most entrepreneurs are very reluctant to part with equity and, in fact, will do whatever they can to avoid it. Handing over equity to a stranger brings a new decision maker into the firm, constrains what they can do and requires them to be accountable. Most would prefer to avoid all three of those situations. Instead, if they need funds, they would rather borrow the money. But what they often fail to recognise is that lenders are highly risk averse and will call in the loan when times get tough.

What many entrepreneurs fail to appreciate are the risks associated with borrowing. They see the interest rate as a minor expense rather than the risk of non payment. Because entrepreneurial firms are somewhat unstable, the chances of falling into a cash vacuum are always present. It only takes a shortage of sales to find the firm short of incoming cash while, at the same time, expenses are eating into available funds. Therefore, the chances of not being able to meet even the interest payments, let alone the capital repayments, should not be underestimated. When that happens, the entire loan can be called in. Few firms can survive such a situation. You should avoid the risk of borrowing whenever you can.

87. Develop Networks

Successful entrepreneur are very good at networking. To some it is instinctive, for others, they work at it. The good ones know that a lot of business is done informally whether it is recruiting staff, finding professional service providers, seeking our suppliers or strategic partners or connecting with prospects. Basically, your connections help you become more effective in business.

The most effective networkers are the connectors. They recall what you do and what things you are interested in and then connect you with another in their network. This way they provide help to people in their network. At the same time, this service is recognized and often returned.

As an emerging company, we don't have the depth of resources of the large corporations, so having a network can dramatically reduce the cost of doing business and speed up problem solving. If I can go to my network to find a supplier or access specialized help, it greatly adds to my ability to manage my business and to grow and prosper. But you have to be an active networker. It won't happen unless you put yourself out there and work at it.

88. Create Good Job Descriptions

Employees need a level of certainty in their roles in order to know they are doing the right thing and that their contributions will be recognized. But if you don't give them clear instructions as to what their role is, what is expected of them and how they will be evaluated, you are creating unnecessary stress in their lives.

We should start recruiting with a good job description which sets out the roles and responsibilities of the job. It should indicate who the person reports to and how the performance of the job will be evaluated. Not only does this set the right expectations internally but it greatly aids in recruiting and selecting the right person. They also know from the outset whether the job is right for them. Longer term, a good job description makes it easier to identify and deal with poor performance, reward good performance and identify those for promotion. We do our employees no favours by neglecting to clearly state what is expected of them.

89. Benchmark Your Business

If you are making reasonable profits and meeting your internally set targets, you might think you are doing well. However, you might be able to do better. What if you could measure yourself against other firms in your industry to identify how well you are really doing? The purpose of benchmarking is to compare the performance of each firm in the benchmarking study to all other firms surveyed. Each firm contributes their own performance across a wide range of activities and in return, finds out how their performance measures up to the rest.

What they find out is what they do well, mediocre and poorly. This allows them to identify where they are falling down in areas where, clearly, other firms are outperforming them. The good news is that, if many other firms are doing better in a specific area, then the reasons should be fairly obvious and action can be taken to improve the situation. Even if we seem to be doing well, we can never afford to be complacent and we need to constantly strive to improve our performance. Benchmarking provides us with a systematic way of uncovering areas for attention. It also forces us to put in place activity measurements across the firm which in itself is a useful management discipline.

90. Measure Customer Satisfaction

You need to ask your customers what they think about your products and services. The key to high growth is satisfied customers. This results in repeat sales, referrals, a positive reputation and employees who are appreciated and therefore more productive as a result. But this shouldn't be guesswork. You need to actually take the effort to periodically check with your customers to ensure you are meeting their requirements. It is very easy for a company to become complacent and gradually lose its way through over confidence. Every now and then you need to collect the evidence to show you are on track.

What you will find is that not everything is being done correctly. There will always be situations which were not performed well, customers who did not have the best experience or products which did not quite live up to their reputation. The key is to find out so you can do something about it. On the other hand, positive feedback can be shared across the organization. Employees like to know they are doing well, especially in the eyes of their customers. You can also use customer surveys to find out how you could further improve your products and services and what else you could do which they would value.

91. Watch Out For The Large Customer

Salespeople love to chase the large deal. They want the big commission, the status and the reputation. But they don't see the risk for the business. Far too often you hear of a small firm losing a major contract and getting into trouble. If you end up committing a significant part of your business to one customer, you are dependent on them for your profitability, if not your survival. If suddenly you lose the contract, you are left with all the fixed costs which you now have to cover from somewhere else.

Big businesses are not known for being kind. They can be entirely ruthless when it comes to suppliers. For them, you are a transaction and the cheaper they can get the business the better. If someone else comes along with a cheaper deal, they will jump ship. At other times, their decision to switch may have nothing to do with the quality of your work. They may be required to do so by a corporate preferred supplier deal. The purchasing manager may have a separate personal agenda to use another supplier or it might be that they simply want to have a change. The bottom line, you can never guarantee they will be your customer in the future. You need to plan accordingly.

92. Raising Funds Takes A Long Time

The last time I raised venture capital it took over nine months and over seventy presentations in most of the major cities along the eastern seaboard of the US. Every fund I went to said that I had an outstanding proposition but even then, it still seemed to take forever. While they were all interested, in the end their decisions were made on whether the investment suited their industry preferences, stage of investing, location of our firm and size of the investment. We did raise the funds eventually but it was a long haul.

I have seen many really good ventures struggle to raise funds. They end up doing endless presentations, attending many meetings and even enter into due diligence only to be rejected. The problem lies not with the firm or the investment proposition but with the preferences of the investor. Basically, until you find someone who has experience in your sector or who is comfortable investing in your sector, you won't see the money. That being the case, you really need to plan your business as if you won't be successful in fund raising.

93. Educate Yourself

Entrepreneurial talent is innate. You only have to spend time with large numbers of entrepreneurs to see the common characteristics. They demonstrate passion, energy, doggedness, optimism, risk taking and a unique creativity to see business opportunities. However, this innate talent does not extend to business acumen. They may see the opportunity but that does not mean they have the basic business skills to execute on it. Since most entrepreneurs who start ventures don't have business training, one of the major factors in the high rate of failure of early stage business is this lack of business education.

You owe it to yourself and to those who depend on your leadership to gain some level of appreciation for business processes. Whether you undertake a formal program or just use your time reading business literature and going to workshops and seminars, you should not underestimate the impact of acquiring a basic understanding of management, marketing, finance and operations management. Most entrepreneurs learn by their mistakes but this is an incredibly wasteful and risky strategy. There are many good books, magazines and business websites where the information is available. Many entrepreneurs associations run education programs for members and there are numerous seminars available on specialist topics to help you develop better business knowledge.

94. Loyalty Is Often Only Skin Deep

One of the saddest things to recognize in business is that employees will leave you when the going gets tough no matter how well you have treated them. It seems that the loyalty which you expected for providing them with a job doesn't extend to helping out when the going gets a little hard. Whether it is pressure on the business from success or setbacks, it doesn't seem to take much to wobble some employees.

Security of employment is very high on the priorities of most employees and you can understand them being concerned about their livelihood if the business gets into trouble. But when things are going well and the future looks bright, it is amazing that some will bail out at that point when they are asked to dig a little deeper and help the business cope with excess work.

We need to be very sensitive to what we ask of people. There are those who will step up and make an extra effort and bear additional stress when things are tough. But there are others who can't handle the extra workload or stress or are simply unwilling to do so. Sad as it may seem, you can't depend on their loyalty even if you feel you have done the right thing by them.

95. Salespeople Always Want More

Your average salesperson is never satisfied with what they have to sell or with the sales collateral they have to work with. For them, it is always the features you don't have which lose them the sale or the brochure which you decided not to commission which caused them to lose a prospect. I have rarely met a salesperson who accepted what they had and did the best they could with what was available to them at that point in time.

What is amazing is that they often complain about things which no one else has. It is not as if they are losing sales to a competitor with better features or better sales material, often it is that they simply want to have more to make their lives easier.

One of the hardest tasks of any entrepreneur is to get the sales staff to sell what you have right now. You need them to sell the product you have today with whatever support you can currently muster and not be always looking over the horizon waiting for what might be coming. You do need to be firm otherwise you won't make the targets you set.

96. Beware Of The Tax Department

It is very tempting to use supplier credit to fund the business but there are some suppliers you don't play games with. One of those is the tax authority. While they may be willing to give some concessions in times of national emergency or natural disasters, in normal times they can be ruthless. You always have to remember that they have more power than you and they have very big sticks to use when they want to get their way.

You have to plan your tax liability very carefully and ensure you can meet your obligation at the time it is due. Just because there is a delay between collecting the cash and paying the tax, this is no excuse for using the money and not being sure of having it on time to pay the tax bill. They won't take that kindly and have been known to shut businesses for non payment.

Also be very careful you don't spend your waking hours trying to find fancy ways to minimise your tax using overseas tax havens, offshore trusts and fancy corporate structures. In the end, the key to success is generating more revenue and executing well on your customer commitments. You will always be more successful in the long run concentrating on making your business more successful than trying to avoid your tax obligations.

97. Build A Reputation

Good reputations make a difference. Whether it is making a sale, recruiting a new employee or selecting a service provider, what people in your industry think about you counts. Think of reputation building as a long term strategy, it doesn't have to be done immediately and in fact can't be. Reputations are imposed on us by others because of what we do and especially, how we do it. If you treat people well, provide good products and services and deal honestly with customers and suppliers, a positive reputation will gradually emerge.

However, you can be proactive in building your reputation. You can be active in industry forums, exhibitions and conferences. You can participate in local and industry charity events. Sponsoring local charities or sporting clubs can grow your reputation in the local community. Public relations is generally free and you should use it to showcase your successes, especially significant achievements and industry awards.

Good reputations are especially useful when it comes to competing for large contracts, getting assistance from local and national governments or asking competitors to join you in industry lobbying. Also, when you come to sell your business, it can make a big difference to the support you garner inside the buying organization.

98. Avoid Litigation Whenever Possible

I know only too well how tempting it is to resort to litigation when you are at an impasse. However, my own experience and that of many entrepreneurs I have discussed this topic with is that, inevitably, the only ones who win are the lawyers. No matter how convinced you are that you are in the right, it is amazing how many times some technicality will destroy your case. Witnesses have dreadful memories, documents are lost, people leave your employment and lawyers move on and you end up with no case or have to start over again. The system seems to conspire against you.

You need to plan your business as much as possible to avoid ever getting into a situation where you need to go to litigation either to bring a case or defend yourself. You need good agreements with suppliers, customers, employees and partners. Your agreements should spell out the rules of engagement and what you expect of each party. You should include mechanisms to ensure you identify problems quickly. Wherever possible, deal with serious problems personally and keep the lawyers out of the picture to give yourself a chance to find an acceptable solution. Always remember, if you are not successful, you could do serious damage to your business. Sometimes it is better to settle or walk away.

99. Empathy Not Excuses

Far too often the response to a mistake is 'Oops Sorry!' which is actually not what the customer wants to hear. They don't want excuses, which only makes the situation worse. What they want is for you to understand the position you put them in and to understand the issues they are dealing with because of your mistake or failure. So the correct response should have been 'I can understand why you feel the way you do'. Basically, we have to put ourselves in the shoes of the customer to experience the pain or problems which they are dealing with. We need to fully comprehend the magnitude of the impact of our mistake.

Once we understand their position, we are in a much better position to offer a solution, correct a deficiency or compensate them for the trouble or expense they have been put through. Not all customers want compensation, sometimes they just want the opportunity to be heard, to voice their complaint and to offer a suggestion. Providing the response they receive is one of sympathy and empathy, most problems will not require any other action on the part of the supplier. How we handle problems says a lot about our values and the importance we place on good customer relations. In the end, our reputation will be greatly impacted by the way in which we handle mistakes.

100. What If There Is No Right Answer

Life would be very easy if the right answer to a problem or situation was always clear cut but unfortunately there are many times in business where this is not the case. Most decisions are easy and obvious. Many situations relate to legal or regulatory obligations and those are easy to deal with. Others are clear cut decisions relating to revenue and expenses and people agree on the solution, However, what do you do when the answer is not obvious, there are several possible solutions but there is no agreement on which should be followed. This often happens in situations where the choices are more moral or ethical and where the decision on what to do depends on your values rather than business logic.

Image you have to cut back on staff numbers and you have to choose which of several good quality staff to retrench. On what basis do you make the decision; least qualified, last in, youngest, most able to find alternative employment and so on. If you asked your management team to decide you may well get a number of conflicting answers. Life as an entrepreneur will throw up these types of decisions and there are no rules to help you apart from being true to your set of values. In the end, you and only you must make the decision and then you have to live with the consequences.

101. The Buck Stops Here

The bottom line for the entrepreneur is that they bear the fruits of their endeavor, whether that be rewards for success or losses for failure. If you step out of your comfort zone and take the risk of undertaking a commercial venture, you should be recognized for the contribution you make. You create employment, pay taxes, contribute to your community and take responsibility for the livelihoods of those you employ. There are few who are willing to do so. Most people would rather have the security of a job (if that can be said to be secure) and allow someone else to look after them and take the risk.

If you are successful, you should be rewarded. Many fail along the way but that is the price for having a go. Most entrepreneurs would rather have a go and take the risk than work for someone else. They want to create their own future not have one handed to them or imposed upon them. The rewards for taking such risks should be non-trivial because we need people to step up, create new enterprises and enrich our economy. If this means we end up creating many more millionaires along the way, that is a worthwhile outcome.

Our entrepreneurs create jobs, contribute to our national wealth, enhance our export capacity and contribute generously to charities. It is a worthwhile pursuit for anyone who wants to make a difference. If, along the way, you make yourself wealthy, then you will have certainly earned the rewards for your effort.

KINDLE BOOKS BY DR. TOM MCKASKILL

Masterclass for Entrepreneurs Series

The Masterclass series is a collection of books each comprising a set of articles published by Dr. McKaskill on a specific topic. These articles have been published in a range of business journals and/or e-business websites.

Masterclass for Entrepreneurs on Fundamentals: Insights into the world of the entrepreneur. (47 pages)

Masterclass for Entrepreneurs on Business Growth: Insights on how to achieve higher growth in your business. (174 pages)

Masterclass for Entrepreneurs on Business Resilience: Insights on how to achieve greater stability, predictability and resilience in your business. (98 pages)

Masterclass for Entrepreneurs on Financial Exits: Insights on how to sell your business to achieve higher EBIT multiples (140 pages)

Masterclass for Entrepreneurs on Strategic Exits: Insights on how to leverage strategic value to achieve a very high price when selling a business. (115 pages)

Masterclass for Entrepreneurs on Angel Finance: Insights on how to successfully fund early stage ventures. (80 pages)

Masterclass for Entrepreneurs on Angel Investing: Insights on how to develop successful angel investing outcomes. (88 pages)

Masterclass for Entrepreneurs on Acquisitions: Insights on developing a successful acquisition process. (108 pages)

Masterclass for Entrepreneurs on the Initial Public Offering: Insights on using an IPO as a funding and exit strategy. (60 pages)

Entrepreneurial Practice Series

In depth books examining best practice in specific processes which are key to the success of an entrepreneurial venture.

Entrepreneurs: The Rollercoaster Ride (165 pages)

Venture Growth Strategies: A practical guide to engineer high growth into an entrepreneurial venture. (157 pages)

Financial Exits: Sell your business for a high EBIT multiple. (170 pages)

Strategic Exits: Leverage strategic assets to sell your business for a very high price. (182 pages)

Raising Angel Finance: Securing private equity funding for early stage firms. (140 pages)

Angel Investing in Early Stage Ventures: A guide to selecting and managing investments. (153 pages)

Creating an Acquisition Strategy: An entrepreneur's guide to pre-acquisition processes. (155 pages)

Managing a New Acquisition: An entrepreneur's guide to post-acquisition processes. (87 pages)

Invest to Exit: A pragmatic strategy for Angel and Venture Capital investors. (251) pages)